W9-AHT-321

Ecosystems
Fresh Waters

Linda Aspen-Baxter

www.av2books.com

AV² provides enriched content that supplements and complements this book. Weigl's AV² books strive to create inspired learning and engage young minds in a total learning experience.

Your AV² Media Enhanced books come alive with...

Audio
Listen to sections of the book read aloud.

Key Words
Study vocabulary, and complete a matching word activity.

Go to **www.av2books.com**, and enter this book's unique code.

Video
Watch informative video clips.

Quizzes
Test your knowledge.

BOOK CODE

Q538851

Embedded Weblinks
Gain additional information for research.

Slide Show
View images and captions, and prepare a presentation.

AV² by Weigl brings you media enhanced books that support active learning.

Try This!
Complete activities and hands-on experiments.

... and much, much more!

Published by AV² by Weigl
350 5th Avenue, 59th Floor
New York, NY 10118
Website: www.av2books.com   www.weigl.com

Library of Congress Cataloging-in-Publication Data

Aspen-Baxter, Linda.
 Fresh waters / Linda Aspen-Baxter.
    p. cm. -- (Ecosystems)
Includes index.
 ISBN 978-1-61913-071-5 (hard cover : alk. paper) -- ISBN 978-1-61913-234-4 (soft cover : alk. paper)
1. Freshwater ecology--Juvenile literature. I. Title.
 QH541.5.F7A87 2013
 577.63--dc23
                          2011044150

Printed in the United States of America in North Mankato, Minnesota
1 2 3 4 5 6 7 8 9 16 15 14 13 12

012012
WEP060112

Project Coordinator Aaron Carr
Design Sonja Vogel

Every reasonable effort has been made to trace ownership and to obtain permission to reprint copyright material. The publishers would be pleased to have any errors or omissions brought to their attention so that they may be corrected in subsequent printings.

Photo Credits
Weigl acknowledges Getty Images as its primary photo supplier for this title.

Contents

AV² Book Code 2

What is a Freshwater Ecosystem? 4

Where in the World? 6

Mapping Rivers and Lakes. 8

Freshwater Climates. 10

Types of Fresh Waters. 12

Freshwater Features. 13

Life in Fresh Waters 14

Freshwater Plants 16

Birds and Mammals 18

Fish, Reptiles, Insects, and Amphibians . . 20

Fresh Waters in Danger. 22

Science in Fresh Waters. 24

Working on the Water 26

Walking on Water 28

Create a Food Web 29

Eco Challenge 30

Glossary/Index 31

Log on to www.av2books.com 32

What is a Freshwater Ecosystem?

Mountain rivers are very fast and cold. Plants and animals must be hardy to survive their rushing waters.

Earth is home to millions of different **organisms**, all of which have specific survival needs. These organisms rely on their environment, or the place where they live, for their survival. All plants and animals have relationships with their environment. They interact with the environment itself, as well as the other plants and animals within the environment. These interactions create **ecosystems**.

The world's fresh waters are a key component of its ecosystems. Precipitation is key to creating and maintaining freshwater ecosystems. When rain and snow fall, some is absorbed by the ground. Water that is not absorbed flows over land and collects in streams, rivers, and lakes. These waterways form an interconnected system that provides habitat for a wide variety of organisms.

Fresh waters support some of the most vibrant ecosystems on the planet. Many **species** have **adapted** to the wide variety of wetland conditions, from seasonal Arctic bogs, to the warm, murky waters of the Amazon River.

Levels of Organization in Freshwater Ecosystems

Organizing Fresh Waters

Ecosystems can be broken down into levels of organization. These levels range from a single organism to many species of organism living together in an area.

Population
Many organisms of the same species

Organism
A single organism

Community
Several species living together

Biosphere
Planet Earth and all of its living things

Ecosystem
Many species of plants and animals in an area

Where in the World?

The fisheries of the African Great Lakes are crucial to the well-being of the people who live nearby.

Rivers, streams, lakes, and ponds are found on every continent. Land regions that were once covered by **glaciers**, such as those found in the Northern **Hemisphere** and in mountain regions, have the highest number of lakes and ponds. However, freshwater ecosystems can be found in other parts of the world as well. Most of the land in South America was never covered by glaciers, so fewer lakes are found on that continent. Instead, many streams and rivers flow downward from higher land into the Amazon River.

Great Lakes

Located in North America, Lake Superior is one of the five lakes known as the Great Lakes. It straddles the Canada–United States border. Lake Superior covers the largest surface area of any freshwater lake in the world. Its area is 31,700 square miles (82,103 square kilometers). Lake Victoria in Africa is the second largest lake in the world. It covers 26,838 square miles (69,510 sq. km). Lakes Malawi, Tanganyika, and Victoria form the African Great Lakes.

Eco Facts

Lake Baikal in Siberia is the world's oldest, deepest lake. It is 25 million years old. Lake Baikal is 1 mile (1.6 km) deep and holds one-fifth of the fresh water on Earth.

The Longest Rivers

Egypt's Nile River is the longest river on Earth. It is 4,145 miles (6,670 km) long. The second longest is the Amazon River in Brazil at 4,000 miles (6,437 km) in length.

Boats can travel along more than 1,172 miles (1,886 km) of Australia's Murray River. Only the Nile and Amazon Rivers have more water accessible to boats.

Mapping Rivers and Lakes

Freshwater rivers and lakes are dominant features on many of Earth's continents. This map shows where the world's largest lakes are located, as well as its important rivers. Find the place where you live on the map. Do you live close to any of these large freshwater systems?

Legend

- Ocean
- Lake
- River

Scale at Equator

```
0        1,000      2,000      3,000 miles
0      1,000      2,000    3,000 kilometers
```

N

ARCTIC OCEAN

Great Bear Lake
Canada

Mackenzie River
Canada

Great Slave Lake
Canada

Lake Winnipeg
Canada

NORTH AMERICA

St. Lawrence River
United States and Canada

ATLANTIC OCEAN

Missouri River
United States

Mississippi River
United States

Rio Grande
United States and Mexico

Lake Maracaibo
Venezuela

SOUTH AMERICA

Lake Titicaca
Bolivia, Peru

PACIFIC OCEAN

SOUTHER OCEAN

Great Lakes

Location: North America (United States, Canada)
Surface Area: 94,000 square miles (243,459 sq. km)
Fact: The Great Lakes region is home to 33.5 million people, and thousands of species of plants and animals. Currently, more than 180 species of non-native **aquatic** life have been introduced by human activity.

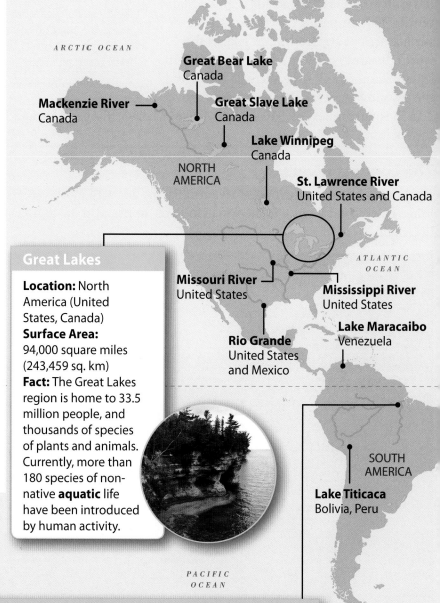

Amazon River

Location: South America (Brazil, Colombia, Ecuador, Peru)
Drainage Basin: 2.7 million square miles (7 million sq. km)
Fact: The Amazon River can be more than 24.8 miles (40 km) wide during the rainy season. It is home to some of the largest freshwater fish on Earth.

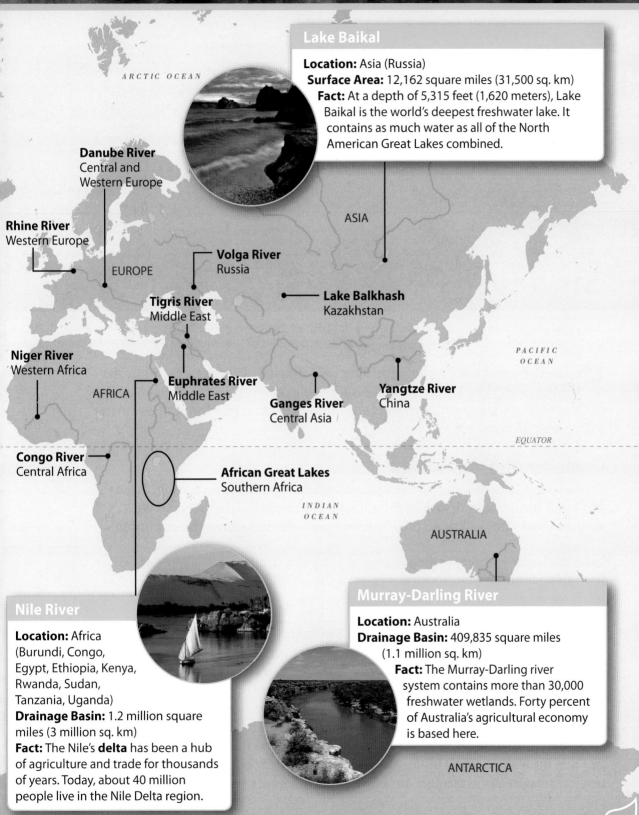

Lake Baikal

Location: Asia (Russia)
Surface Area: 12,162 square miles (31,500 sq. km)
Fact: At a depth of 5,315 feet (1,620 meters), Lake Baikal is the world's deepest freshwater lake. It contains as much water as all of the North American Great Lakes combined.

Danube River
Central and Western Europe

Rhine River
Western Europe

Volga River
Russia

Tigris River
Middle East

Lake Balkhash
Kazakhstan

Niger River
Western Africa

Euphrates River
Middle East

Yangtze River
China

Ganges River
Central Asia

Congo River
Central Africa

African Great Lakes
Southern Africa

ARCTIC OCEAN

ASIA

EUROPE

AFRICA

PACIFIC OCEAN

EQUATOR

INDIAN OCEAN

AUSTRALIA

ANTARCTICA

Nile River

Location: Africa (Burundi, Congo, Egypt, Ethiopia, Kenya, Rwanda, Sudan, Tanzania, Uganda)
Drainage Basin: 1.2 million square miles (3 million sq. km)
Fact: The Nile's **delta** has been a hub of agriculture and trade for thousands of years. Today, about 40 million people live in the Nile Delta region.

Murray-Darling River

Location: Australia
Drainage Basin: 409,835 square miles (1.1 million sq. km)
Fact: The Murray-Darling river system contains more than 30,000 freshwater wetlands. Forty percent of Australia's agricultural economy is based here.

Freshwater Climates

Forty-three percent of Alaska is covered by freshwater wetlands. This accounts for 63 percent of the wetlands in the United States.

Freshwater ecosystems do not have their own climates. They are affected by the land around them. If a river or lake is located in desert country, the climate in the area will be hot and dry. If a river runs through tropical rain forest, the climate will be hot and humid.

Changing With the Seasons

Freshwater regions are affected by seasonal changes in temperate climates. Ponds and small streams may dry up in summer. In winter, ponds may freeze to the bottom. Ponds are shallow, so their temperature is the same from top to bottom.

Lakes are larger and deeper than ponds, so the water temperature is more varied. In summer, the Sun heats the upper layer of the lake. The Sun's heat does not reach the deeper water, so it stays cool.

In autumn, colder weather begins, and the top layer of water cools. Strong winds cause waves, which mix the layers of water. The temperature of the lake water becomes more uniform. In winter, the top layer may cool enough to freeze, forming a layer of ice on top. This ice floats and **insulates** the water underneath from the cold air above it. The ice also stops winter winds from mixing the water. The bottom layer stays relatively warm. In spring, the air temperature warms and thaws the ice on top. The top layer warms in the Sun, and the winds again move and mix the water layers. This mixing happens seasonally in cool climates. In tropical areas, seasonal changes are smaller, and lakes are mixed by wind and rain.

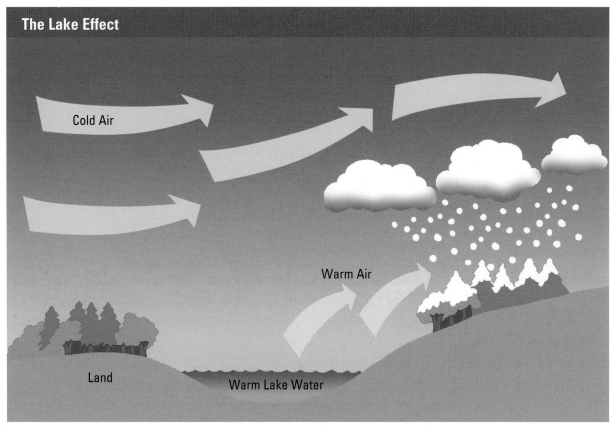

The Lake Effect

Cold Air

Warm Air

Land

Warm Lake Water

Lake-effect snowfall can leave up to 1 foot (30 centimeters) of snow within a few hours.

Lake Effects

Depending on their size, rivers and lakes can also affect the climate. Large bodies of water store heat from the Sun. Water warms and cools more slowly than air. In summer, large rivers and lakes are still cool from winter and spring, and the temperature of the water is cooler than the air. Winds off the lake or river cool the land nearby. This is called the lake effect. In winter, large bodies of water cool off more slowly than the air. This helps keep temperatures around the lake or river warmer in winter.

The air over lakes and rivers contains more moisture than the air over land. This moisture, or water vapor, forms clouds and may fall as precipitation over land. Large lakes can cause heavy snowfalls on nearby land. Air that moves over a large lake becomes moist and warmer. When this air reaches land, it meets colder, drier air. This clash produces lake-effect snow.

Eco Facts

Rivers are earth movers. All of the world's rivers combined remove an average of 2 tons (1.8 tonnes) of rock and soil from every square mile (2.6 sq. km) of land they cross each year.

Types of Fresh Waters

The movement of ice can grind rock into fine dust. When this dust enters lakes, it reflects the Sun's light, giving the water a bright blue or green color.

Lakes and Ponds

Lakes and ponds are inland bodies of standing water. They are found in all types of environments on all seven continents. A pond is small and shallow enough that light can reach right to the bottom. Ponds sometimes form naturally in hollows, or they can result from the building of dams, either by humans or beavers. Lakes are larger and deeper than ponds. They are fed by rivers, springs, or precipitation. Ponds are sometimes seasonal, drying up when hot weather arrives. Lakes can be hundreds, even millions, of years old.

Rivers and Streams

Rivers and streams are bodies of moving water. These bodies of water often originate at springs and lakes. Sometimes, they develop from the melting snow of glaciers. At first, they may be just a trickle of water, but they gradually become larger. Water always follows the downward slope of the land because of the pull of gravity. The flow of the water creates tiny gullies as it flows downward over the surface. These gullies meet and form bigger gullies. When water reaches a valley or has enough steady flow to create its own channel, it becomes a stream. Some streams flow only when it rains or when warm weather melts parts of glaciers. Other streams flow all year. Streams join together to form small rivers. When small rivers join a larger river, they are called tributaries. This network of streams and rivers forms a **watershed**, which drains excess water from the land.

Eco Facts

The world's largest delta straddles the border of India and Bangladesh. It is formed by the Ganges and Brahmaputra Rivers. The Ganges delta is approximately the same size as the entire country of Scotland.

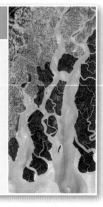

Freshwater Features

T he force of a river or stream moves **sediment** and causes **erosion**. These processes create new landforms and change the flow of the water. Deltas, waterfalls, and rapids are just a few examples of how water charts its own course.

Deltas

A river's mouth is the place where the river empties into another body of water. As the water flows toward the mouth, it slows down. The sediment and mud that it carries sink to the bottom of the river, creating deposits. As more mud and sediment gathers, the deposits grow and become new land. This type of land formation is called a delta. Water that once flowed straight splits into smaller channels across the width of the delta.

Waterfalls

Waterfalls tend to form close to the source of a river, usually on a hill or mountain. The water here typically moves faster than on flat land. This fast-moving water travels over both hard and soft rock. Over time, the force of the water erodes the soft rock. This erosion can cut a sharp drop in the rock, creating a waterfall.

Rapids

Much like a waterfall, rapids occur when a fast-moving river flows down a slope. The drop is not as great as that of a waterfall, and the water is usually more shallow. The current is still strong, however, and the water foams around the many rocks it encounters.

A reas rich in fresh water are often lush, green, and teeming with life. Freshwater lakes, rivers, and wetlands support a tremendous diversity of fish, plants, birds, and other organisms. These plants and animals depend on each other for the food, or energy, they need to survive. This energy transfers from one organism to another through the food chain.

Producers

The plants found in freshwater environments act as producers for other organisms in the ecosystem. These organisms are called producers because they make their own food. They also serve as food for other organisms. Producers absorb energy from the Sun and convert it into usable forms of energy such as sugar. They make this energy through a process called **photosynthesis**. Producers found in fresh waters include mangrove trees, grasses, and other aquatic plants.

Primary Consumers

The animals that rely on producers as a food source are called primary consumers. When a primary consumer feeds on a producer, the energy made by the producer is transferred to the consumer. Examples of primary consumers found in freshwater ecosystems include insects, small fish, and even larger animals such as moose and beavers.

Freshwater Energy Pyramid

The transfer of energy in an ecosystem begins with producers and moves up the energy pyramid to the tertiary consumers. Organisms at each level of the pyramid receive energy from the organisms in the level below them.

Outside of the pyramid are the decomposers. They break down the dead and decaying **organic** matter left behind when plants and animals die. For this reason, decomposers receive energy from organisms in all levels of the energy pyramid.

Tertiary Consumers

Secondary Consumers

Primary Consumers

Producers

Freshwater Food Web

Another way to study the flow of energy through an ecosystem is by examining food chains and food webs. A food chain shows how a producer feeds a primary consumer, which then feeds a secondary consumer, and so on. However, most organisms feed on many different food sources. This practice causes food chains to interconnect, creating a food web.

In this example, the **red line** represents one food chain from the algae to the tadpole and snapping turtle. The blue line from the coontail to the cichlid, kingfisher, and turtle forms another food chain. These food chains connect at the turtle, but they also connect in other places. The cichlid also feeds on algae, and the kingfisher may also eat tadpoles. This series of connections forms a complex food web.

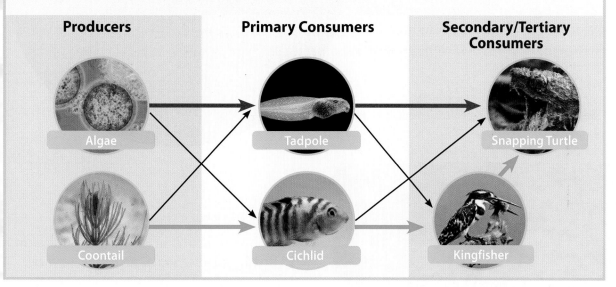

Producers	Primary Consumers	Secondary/Tertiary Consumers
Algae	Tadpole	Snapping Turtle
Coontail	Cichlid	Kingfisher

Secondary and Tertiary Consumers

Secondary consumers feed on both producers and primary consumers. In fresh waters, secondary consumers include reptiles and **amphibians**, such as turtles and frogs. Most birds, some mammals, and even insects such as dragonflies are also secondary consumers. Larger carnivores, such as bears, and some large reptiles, including crocodiles, are called tertiary consumers. Tertiary consumers feed on secondary consumers.

Decomposers

Many types of bacteria and scavenging fish live in freshwater ecosystems. These organisms are called decomposers because they eat dead and decaying organic materials. Decomposers speed up the process of breaking down dead organic materials and releasing their **nutrients** into the water. These nutrients are then absorbed by aquatic plants.

Freshwater Plants

Submergent Plants

Submergent plants grow entirely under the water's surface. Wild celery, coontail, and watermilfoil are just a few examples of submergent plants found in fresh waters. Wild celery is found in coastal freshwater inlets and waterways. It is an important food source for many aquatic birds. Coontail can be found deep under the surface. This plant does not have roots, so it absorbs all of its nutrients from the water instead of the soil. Watermilfoil is a shallow-water plant. Its stems can grow to 6 feet (1.8 m) in length.

Sunlight can only reach 656 feet (200 m) below the water's surface. Past this point, no plants can grow.

Floating Plants

Aquatic plants that live on the water's surface are called floating plants. Some, such as watermeal, float freely and have no roots. Others may have roots that connect them to the ground. The most well-known floating plant is the water lily. The flower of the water lily sits on the surface of the water, while its root is buried in the mud at the bottom of the pond. Duckweed is the smallest flowering plant. It floats on the surface in spring and summer. During this time, it produces extra energy. This energy is stored as a sugary chemical called starch, which weighs the plant down. By autumn, duckweed sinks to the bottom. It uses the extra starch to stay alive during the winter. In spring, duckweed floats back to the surface again.

Duckweed grows in slow-moving or still water. It can be found around the world.

Eco Facts

Fish and waterfowl often find their food on the leaves of coontail. The thick, bushy leaves are ideal living environments for the tiny organisms that fish and birds feed on. Coontail has more food organisms living on its leaves than any other aquatic plant.

Emergent Plants

Emergent plants grow partly in and partly out of the water. Their roots are under the water, and their stems and leaves are at least partly above the water. These plants tend to grow close to the water's edge or in shallow water. Their roots are anchored in the mud beneath the water, while their stems shoot high above the surface. Some plants can grow as much as 6 feet (1.8 m) out of the water. Cattails and bulrushes are some of the most common types of emergent plant found in fresh waters. Cattails are easily recognized by their flowers, which mass together to form a brown spike at the top of each plant. Some species of reeds and grasses can also be emergent plants.

Some emergent plants live in areas called mangroves, where fresh water flows out to sea. The water in mangroves is called brackish, which means it is partly salty.

Birds and Mammals

Waterfowl

Birds such as ducks, geese, and swans, spend most of their time on the water. As a group, they are known as waterfowl. They have webbed feet close to the rear of their bodies to help them swim. They also have flattened bills to grab the plants on which they feed. Ducks have different feeding styles. Dabbling ducks, such as pintails and mallards, stay on the surface and dip their bills to catch tiny animals in the water. Diving ducks, such as scaups and loons, head to deeper waters. They dive deep down into the water to catch fish.

Most waterfowl produce a special oil that coats their feathers. The oil repels water, keeping the birds dry.

A flamingo's food is full of colorful chemicals called pigments. These pigments turn the flamingo pink.

Wading Birds

Wading birds include herons, limpkins, and sunbitterns. These birds have long legs and wide feet for wading in shallow water. They also have long necks and bills shaped like daggers for spearing fish and frogs. Other waders, such as flamingos, have beaks shaped to let them strain tiny shrimp from the water.

Shorebirds

Shorebirds, such as the plover and sandpiper, feed and nest along the banks and shores of lakes, rivers, and ponds. Their bills are shaped to help them get the food they need. The godwit has a long, slender upturned bill for rooting through the mud. The bill of the ruddy turnstone is curved to one side so it can turn over pebbles and shells.

Mammals

Many species of mammal visit streams, rivers, ponds, and lakes in search of food and water. Some mammals live in freshwater ecosystems and spend most of their time in the water. Mammals such as beavers, muskrats, minks, otters, platypuses, and freshwater dolphins make their homes in fresh waters. Many of these mammals have thick, waterproof fur. This keeps them warm and dry, even in very cold water. Some of these mammals also have webbed feet for swimming. Strong, muscular tails help propel them through the water. Even the eyes, ears, and nostrils of these mammals have adapted to life in the water. The Eurasian otter closes its nostrils and ears when it is in the water. The ear and eye openings of the platypus are closed off by folds of skin when the animal is submerged.

Eco Facts

The platypus uses its sensitive bill to probe the mud at the bottom of the water for food. Its bill is able to detect the contractions of its prey's muscles.

Freshwater dolphins send out sound waves that bounce off objects underwater. The sound waves help them find the fish on which they prey.

Beavers often build dams across rivers, forming ponds. Beavers and humans are the only two animals on Earth who do this.

Fish, Reptiles, Insects, and Amphibians

Fish

Fish have perfect body shapes for life underwater. Their streamlined shape helps them move through the water upstream against the current. Their gills allow them to breathe underwater. They can inflate or deflate their swim bladders to adjust their level in the water. Some fish feed on the surface, and some prefer deep water. Trout prefer fast-moving streams. They are small and shaped like torpedoes, so they can swim upstream in search of food. Pike hide in water plants while they watch for prey. Their striped and spotted bodies help them blend into their surroundings. When they see their prey, they dart out to snap it up with their sharp teeth.

Piranhas hunt in large groups. Rarely, several groups will band together to attack large animals.

Reptiles

Many reptiles have adapted to living in water. Southeast Asian fishing snakes can close their nostrils when they are swimming. Gavials, in northern India, have hind legs like paddles to help them swim. They use their long, narrow snouts filled with sharp teeth to snap down on fish and frogs underwater. Some reptiles, like gavials, are carnivores. Others, such as turtles, eat mostly plants. Reptiles are cold-blooded. This means that they rely on warm weather and water to heat their bodies, allowing them to be active. Many **hibernate** when the weather turns cold or become dormant in hot, dry weather.

Nile crocodiles live in fresh waters all over Africa. They can grow up to 20 feet (6 m) in length.

Eco Facts

The African lungfish can actually move over land. When its pond dries up, it uses its fins as legs. It breathes air with simple lungs. If it has to, it can even bury itself in mud and stay dormant until rains return.

The larvae of diving beetles are such skilled hunters that they are called water tigers.

Insects

Insect **larvae** may be small, but they have ways to survive in fresh waters. Black fly larvae have suction cups to help them stick to rocks. For food, they eat tiny creatures that float past them in the current. Mayfly larvae have hooks on their legs for hanging onto algae-covered rocks. Mosquito larvae pull air from plant stems to breathe underwater. Fisher spiders feed on insects and tadpoles. Hairs all over their bodies spread their weight to let them walk on the water's surface. The hairs also trap air, so they can breathe underwater while they hunt. Some insects live their whole lives in the water. Others live in water for only part of their life, living on land when they become adults.

Amphibians

Amphibians live at least part of their lives in water. When they are young, they usually eat aquatic plants. All adult amphibians are carnivores. Frogs begin their lives as jelly-like eggs laid just beneath the surface of the water. When the eggs hatch, tadpoles emerge. Tadpoles have gills, so they can breathe in water. When tadpoles become frogs, they develop lungs, though they still need water to lay their eggs and to keep their skin moist. Frogs have sticky tongues that help them capture their food. Salamanders and newts also begin their lives in a tadpole-like stage. Many lose their gills and live on dry land as adults.

A frog's teeth are curved inward to keep prey from escaping.

One of the most serious problems for freshwater ecosystems is water pollution. Fertilizers, livestock waste, pesticides, and industrial pollution all enter fresh waters through runoff. Some sewage is dumped right into rivers and streams. Sewage and fertilizer can cause bacteria to multiply quickly. Bacteria use up the oxygen in the water, causing aquatic species to die. This phenomenon is responsible for a large "dead zone" in the Gulf of Mexico. Agricultural runoff is collected by the Mississippi River and enters the ocean. This creates an area as large as 7,000 square miles (18,130 sq. km) off the Mississippi Delta where very few organisms can live. Toxic chemicals can also drift to the bottom of lakes and ponds, where they are consumed by small animals. As these animals are eaten by larger ones, the toxins are carried up the food chain. Eventually, tertiary consumers, including people, can become ill.

Development is also a major threat to freshwater ecosystems. Dams are often built to generate power or **irrigate** crops. When these dams divert the flow of a river, the downstream areas may suffer. Wetlands, lakes, and even inland seas can dry up, destroying the habitat of many species. In the 1960s, the Soviet Union diverted many of the rivers that fed the Aral Sea, one of the largest lakes in the world at the time. Since then, the Aral has shrunk by more than 90 percent, killing off many animals, and destroying the livelihood of the people who live there.

Timeline of Human Activity in Fresh Waters

Glaciers covering the northern hemisphere begin to retreat, leaving rifts in the land that will become lakes and rivers.

It is estimated that 60,000 to 117,000 Aboriginal people live in and around the Great Lakes region.

The world's first hydroelectric generating plant opens in Appleton, Wisconsin.

12,000 BC — **3,000 BC** — **1500 AD** — **1541** — **1882** — **1887**

Ancient Egyptians use sailing ships to travel the Nile River and its surrounding waters.

Francisco de Orellana becomes the first European to explore the Amazon River.

North America's first waterfowl refuge is established at Last Mountain Lake in Saskatchewan, Canada.

Plastic does not break down easily in nature. Waste plastic may pollute waterways for centuries to come.

The Australian government begins directly managing the Murray River. Dams, locks, and **weirs** are built to water crops and prevent droughts.

The Clean Water Act goes into effect, creating laws to protect clean, healthy waterways in the United States.

A foreign species of **diatom** is found in New Zealand waters, threatening fragile waterways. It can overgrow ponds and streams, killing off local wildlife.

1918　　**1959**　　**1971**　　**1972**　　**1975**　　**2004**

The St. Lawrence Seaway opens, allowing large ships to reach the Great Lakes from the Atlantic Ocean.

The Convention on Wetlands of International Importance especially as Waterfowl Habitat is signed in Iraq. Today, 133 nations have acknowledged the importance of freshwater ecosystems and taken steps to protect them.

The cargo ship *Edmund Fitzgerald* sinks on Lake Superior, in one of the most famous shipping disasters in the history of the Great Lakes.

Science in Fresh Waters

The Three Gorges Dam on China's Yangtze River produces as much power as 18 coal-burning power plants.

The world's fresh waters are an important source of both water and power. Fresh waters supply drinking water and support the growth of crops throughout the world. They are also used to create hydroelectricity. Household appliances, such as refrigerators and televisions, rely on hydroelectricity for power.

Hydroelectricity

Hydroelectricity is clean, renewable energy, produced through the use of dams. A dam is built across a river to control the flow of water. The stored water becomes a lake or **reservoir**. When released, the water passes through turbines inside the dam. The rushing water spins the blades of these turbines to produce electricity. This type of power does not pollute, but it can cause other environmental problems. Dams must be constructed carefully, in order to avoid damaging the surrounding ecosystems.

The World's Largest Dams

The largest hydroelectric plant in the world is the Three Gorges Dam, in China's Hubei province. It is capable of producing 20,300 megawatts of electricity. By comparison, many nuclear power plants in the United States produce about 3,000 megawatts. Itaipú Dam, on the Paraná River in South America, is the second-largest hydroelectric plant. It has 18 generators that can produce 14,000 megawatts. This provides 94 percent of the electricity used by Paraguay and 20 percent of that used by Brazil.

Eco Facts

Today, more than 848,000 square miles (2.2 million sq. km) of the world's land is irrigated. Almost 70 percent of all the fresh water taken from rivers, lakes, reservoirs, and wells is used for irrigation.

Irrigation

Fresh water is also used to irrigate crops. Many regions of the world are very dry. Irrigation makes it possible to grow crops in dry regions. Different methods of irrigation are used to water crops. Drip irrigation is used with fruits and vegetables. Plastic pipes with holes in them are laid along rows of crops. Water is pumped through the pipes to water the plants.

High-pressure

High-pressure spray irrigation has been the standard way to irrigate crops in North America. A long tube carries water from a pump. All along the tube are triangular frames on wheels. This long arm of frames moves in a circle around the pump. The pump sends water to sprinklers all along the tube.

Low-pressure

Low-pressure spray irrigation is replacing high-pressure irrigation. A large pipe carries water out from a pump in the center. Small water sprayers hang down from this pipe. Each has a nozzle close to the ground that sprays water gently onto the crops. More than 90 percent of the water gets to the crop.

❚ Irrigation accounts for 70 percent of the water used in Australia each year. ❚

Working on the Water

Studying the animals living in fresh waters can teach scientists a great deal about the health of the ecosystem.

People who work in freshwater ecosystems play an important role in maintaining the health of these areas. They work to improve and protect freshwater habitats and find ways for people to use them responsibly. They also learn about the vital role fresh waters play in the environment.

Limnologist

Duties

Studies the plant and animal life that live in freshwater ecosystems

Education

Bachelor of science in biology, ecology, or environmental science

Interests

Aquatic animals and plants, chemistry, conservation, working outdoors

Limnologists study the plants and animals that live in fresh waters. They also study anything that affects the natural balance of these ecosystems. Monitoring the health of lakes, ponds, rivers, and streams is one key duty. This is often done by checking whether numbers of aquatic animals are increasing or decreasing. Limnologists also work on solutions to improve the health of waterways.

Other Freshwater Jobs

Environmental Consultant

Studies ecosystems and determines methods of protecting them, while still allowing responsible human development

Fisheries Officer

Ensures the protection of sensitive freshwater ecosystems by monitoring fishing practices

Water Treatment Specialist

Uses knowledge of chemistry and biology to ensure drinking water is safe and aquatic communities are protected

Ruth Myrtle Patrick

Ruth Myrtle Patrick was born in Topeka, Kansas, in 1907. During walks in the forest with her family, Ruth would collect muck from stream beds and study the tiny creatures that lived there. By 1934, she had pursued her passions to a doctoral degree in botany, granted by the University of Virginia. Patrick was a leader in her field at a time when few other women were active in the sciences.

In the 1940s, Patrick developed a method for testing the health of a freshwater ecosystem. This was done by measuring the different types of plants and animals present in samples. If many different types of organisms are found, this means that the ecosystem is thriving. Using the diversity of an ecosystem to check its health is now known as the "Patrick Principle." In 1947, her innovative ideas led to the founding of the Limnology Department at the Academy of Natural Sciences in Philadelphia. Patrick led this department until 1973.

Patrick's drive and expertise are widely noted by ecologists. In 1973, she became the first woman to chair the Academy of Natural Sciences. She has received 25 honorary degrees from universities around the United States for her conservation and contributions to ecology. In 1996, President Bill Clinton awarded her the National Medal of Science. Speaking of her career, Patrick said, "I have always tried to leave the world a better place through my science."

Walking on Water

Some insects appear to walk on the water's surface. They can do this because of surface tension. Surface tension allows water to hold up things that are heavier and denser than water itself. A drop of water is made of smaller parts called molecules. Water molecules have bonds that hold them together. At the surface of the water, water molecules bind more easily to each other than to the air above. This difference in strength forms an invisible "skin" called surface tension. Try this experiment to see how surface tension works.

Materials

Kitchen Pan   **Water**   **Dish Soap**   **Black Pepper**   **Toothpicks**

1. Fill the pan halfway with water. Gently sprinkle the black pepper on top. Most of it should float.

2. Using a clean toothpick, touch the surface of the water, and observe the results.

3. Dip a toothpick into the dish soap, and use it to touch the surface of the water. What happened differently?

Results

The clean toothpick should have produced no effect. When the dish soap came in contact with the water, you likely saw the pepper move rapidly toward the sides of the pan. Molecules in the soap bind with the water. In fact, they bind to the soap more strongly than to other water molecules. This causes the soap to be drawn across the water. As the soap spreads across the surface of the water, the pepper is carried with it.

Create a Food Web

U se this book and research on the Internet to create a food web of freshwater ecosystem producers and consumers. Start by finding at least three organisms of each type—producers, primary consumers, secondary consumers, and tertiary consumers. Then, begin linking these organisms together into food chains. Draw the arrows of each food chain in a different color. Use a **red** pen or crayon for one food chain and green and blue for the others. You should find that many of these food chains connect, creating a food web. Add the rest of the arrows to complete the food web using a pencil or **black** pen.

Once your food web is complete, use it to answer the following questions.

1 How would removing one organism from your food web affect the other organisms in the web?

2 What would happen to the rest of the food web if the producers were taken away?

3 How would decomposers fit into the food web?

Sample Food Web

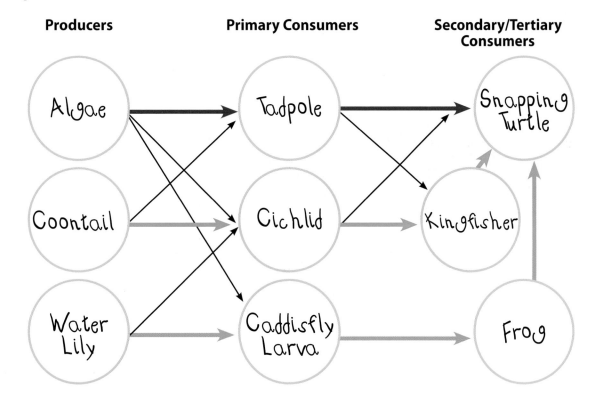

Producers — Primary Consumers — Secondary/Tertiary Consumers

Algae, Coontail, Water Lily, Tadpole, Cichlid, Caddisfly Larva, Snapping Turtle, Kingfisher, Frog

Eco Challenge

1. Which hemisphere has the greatest number of lakes and ponds?

2. Which freshwater lake covers the most surface area?

3. What causes warm and cool layers of lake water to mix?

4. Why does water follow the downward slope of the land?

5. What substance, deposited as rivers enter lakes and oceans, creates deltas?

6. Which type of aquatic plant grows completely under the water?

7. What is one adaptation shared by waterfowl and some mammals that helps them swim?

8. Name at least two insects whose life cycles begin in water.

9. Which group of animals lose their gills as they reach adulthood?

10. What is the most serious problem that endangers freshwater ecosystems?

Answers

1. Northern Hemisphere
2. Lake Superior
3. Wind
4. It follows the force of gravity
5. Sediment
6. Submergent
7. Webbed feet
8. Mosquitoes and dragonflies
9. Amphibians
10. Water pollution

Glossary

adapted: changed to fit the environment

amphibians: cold-blooded animals that live all or part of their lives in water

aquatic: living or growing in, on, or near the water

delta: an area of land at the mouth of a river

diatom: a tiny, plantlike organism

ecosystems: communities of living things sharing an environment

erosion: the process of wearing away

glaciers: masses of ice formed from snow falling over a long period of time

hemisphere: one of two halves of Earth

hibernate: to spend the winter in a sleeplike state

insulates: covers with a material that slows or stops heat or cold

irrigate: to water dry land using pipes or ditches

larvae: the newly hatched, wingless form of many insects

nutrients: substances that feed plants or animals

organic: made up of living things

organisms: living things

photosynthesis: the process in which a green plant uses sunlight to change water and carbon dioxide into food for itself

reservoir: an artificial or human-made lake

sediment: fine material that settles to the bottom of a liquid

species: a group of similar animals that can mate together

watershed: the area drained by a river or stream

weirs: low dams, built to control the flow of a river or stream

Index

amphibians 15, 21, 30

birds 14, 15, 17, 18

climate 10, 11

delta 9, 12, 13, 22, 30

erosion 13

fish 8, 14, 15, 17, 18, 19, 20, 21

glaciers 6, 12, 22

hydroelectricity 22, 24, 25

insects 14, 15, 21, 28, 30

irrigation 22, 25

lake effect 11

mammals 15, 19, 30

plants 4, 5, 8, 14, 15, 16, 17, 18, 20, 21, 24, 25, 27, 30

pollution 22, 23, 24, 30

precipitation 4, 11, 12

reptiles 15, 20

reservoir 24, 25

Log on to www.av2books.com

AV² by Weigl brings you media enhanced books that support active learning. Go to www.av2books.com, and enter the special code found on page 2 of this book. You will gain access to enriched and enhanced content that supplements and complements this book. Content includes video, audio, weblinks, quizzes, a slide show, and activities.

Audio
Listen to sections of the book read aloud.

Video
Watch informative video clips.

Embedded Weblinks
Gain additional information for research.

Try This!
Complete activities and hands-on experiments.

WHAT'S ONLINE?

Try This!	Embedded Weblinks	Video	EXTRA FEATURES
Complete an activity to test your knowledge of the levels of organization in a freshwater ecosystem.	Find out more information on freshwater ecosystems.	Watch a video about freshwater ecosystems.	**Audio** Listen to sections of the book read aloud.
Complete an activity to test your knowledge of energy pyramids.	Learn more about the animals that live in freshwater ecosystems.	Watch a video about animals that live in freshwater ecosystems.	**Key Words** Study vocabulary, and complete a matching word activity.
Create a timeline of important events in freshwater ecosystems.	Find out more about the plants that grow in freshwater ecosystems.		
Write a biography about a scientist.	Read about current research in freshwater ecosystems.		**Slide Show** View images and captions, and prepare a presentation.
	Learn more about threats facing freshwater ecosystems.		**Quizzes** Test your knowledge.

AV² was built to bridge the gap between print and digital. We encourage you to tell us what you like and what you want to see in the future.

Sign up to be an AV² Ambassador at www.av2books.com/ambassador.